# The River

Richard L. Boyd

RICHARD BOYD

# FORWARD

These are stories about the Susquehanna River that I have been told, read about, and experienced.

The Susquehanna is the longest river on the East Coast that empties into the Atlantic Ocean. The north branch of the river begins near Cooperstown, NY, as the outlet for Otsego Lake. It flows for 444 miles through New York state, Pennsylvania and enters the northern portion of the Chesapeake Bay at Havre de Grace, Maryland.

Counting rivers, streams, creeks and other tributaries, it has more than 49,000 miles of waterways.

I was born Nov. 27, 1924, and began to learn about the Susquehanna River and its tributaries at an early age — really as soon as I could walk. Over the years I have fished the river from Goldsboro, just south of Harrisburg in Pennsylvania, to the mouth of the river in Havre de Grace, where tidal waters become the Chesapeake Bay, flowing to the Atlantic. I always found the river and its islands and waterways fascinating.

My father, Howard L. Boyd, loved fishing and the Susquehanna River. I learned to fish in all types of weather, sometimes with ice frozen in the eyelets of the rods, and the line frozen stiff. When it was that cold we collected driftwood, splitting it or breaking it by hand, to build a bonfire on the riverbank to help me stay warm.

I really never complained: Cold weather, rainy weather, windy weather, hot weather, just get me and my dad and family at the river. Dad's family was especially addicted to the water.

Dick Boyd

RICHARD BOYD

# PART ONE — THE RIVER

## Spring on the Susquehanna

Spring always began along the river with the bugs we knew as the shad fly, which are also called mayflies. When I was young, they swarmed in the millions. If we were fishing at night and using a lantern, they would swarm to the light and cover it so we couldn't see except through their wings and bodies.

The dogwood, shadbush, and bloodroot all bloomed along the river during this time. It was beautiful and picturesque in its own way. The river shoreline and its banks were wild and unspoiled.

In the early years, man and machine hadn't really arrived yet and the sound of a power lawnmower never reached the riverbanks.

Fishermen once knew that when the shad flies arrived the shad fish weren't far behind. But the dams along the lower Susquehanna changed all that and the shad never arrived.

## Fishing Near York Haven

The story of the Susquehanna River is also a story of its reservoirs and dams. One of the early dams was a stone diversion angled across the river to the first hydroelectric plant at York Haven.

This first dam along the lower Susquehanna, built in 1904, is 12 miles south of Harrisburg. At the time it was built it was third-largest dam in the world. It still stands, a wing-angled dam that is nearly a mile long, backing up water to form Lake Frederick. It still produces 20 megawatts of electricity.

Many years ago you could take a small wooden boat, as I did, up to the breast of the dam. It was made of huge boulders. How they got them in place there, I never understood.

However, a paper mill had the first water rights from that stone dam. If the flow became too low, the power company had to shut the electric-generating turbines down and serve the paper mill first. The paper mill was closed after a flood in the 1970s and the rights for the dam water flow then belonged to the electric power company.

My experience fishing the waters of the Susquehanna was generally below the dam at York Haven. I spent a great deal of time along the banks of the tailrace where the water flowed from the paper mill.

The water here was very swift and we didn't use sinkers. Instead we went to our metal scrap pile and tied old washers, nuts and bolts to our fishing lines with what we called cord string. In that water you never got your sinker back unless you caught a fish, and we never had any money to buy lead sinkers.

This was during the Depression, and we caught fish for food. We never threw a fish back that was big enough to eat, unless the fish we caught was out of season. These were bass and walleyes; or as we called them, Susquehanna salmon.

The fish we caught in the tailrace were mullets and a few catfish. Sometimes we could catch a few below the power dam when the river was high and swift.

Another good fishing area was what we called "the point." That was a little stony area at the end of the power plant, perhaps 50 square feet. Conewago Creek entered the river next to the tailrace from the paper plant. Next to the point upriver the water turned the turbines, generating electricity. The power plant seldom had all the turbines on at the same time, and the river level rose or fell according to how many were turned on. The more turbines turned on, the swifter the river.

There were many large rocks in the river near the point. Once Dad rented a boat — no motor, just two wooden oars. Mother was with us that day and we were fishing for Susquehanna salmon, which meant we rowed around the river fishing with a silver spoon, a night crawler and a small sinker.

That day Dad was rowing and Mother and I were fishing. We hit a submerged rock, and it spun us around like a top, over and over. The power plant had opened more turbines, or as we called them, "the gates." That changed the flow of the river. As the water level rose we floated away from the rock. I was too young to be scared. The amazing thing is we didn't quit fishing, though I can't remember what we caught that day.

Many times we went out to the point and fished all day and night. We caught a lot of fish; Susquehanna salmon (our favorite), bass, catfish, and a species we called silver carp.

There was a strange animal that we caught and named waterdogs. They had a skin like a catfish, a head similar to a catfish, large upper and lower teeth and four legs. That was the only place I ever caught any the entire length of the river that I fished. We never brought any home; we always killed them. They grew up to 16 inches long.

Why we killed them, I was never told. We caught them using live minnows. I never heard anyone back then tell me what they were. I often wished I knew where they came from and how they got there, as well as what happened to them.

It turns out they are also called mudpuppies, and they are the larval form of a kind of salamander. They live on the bottoms of lakes, ponds, rivers and in the United States and they range from the East Coast and Midwest. "Fishermen who hook mudpuppies will often cut their line rather than touch these extremely slimy amphibians, believing incorrectly that they are poisonous," according to National Geographic.

At the mouth of the Conewago Creek, where it entered the Susquehanna, one of the industries in the York Haven area dumped its coal ashes into the creek and created what we called a cinder bar. I fished a lot off the bar. It was a great place to catch big old mud carp, lots of catfish and a few bass.

# Camping With Granddad

One year when I was very young, my dad took his dad — my grandfather — and me up to York Haven camping for a week. He left my grandpa and me on an island by ourselves. This was Brunner Island, which lay between Conewago Creek and the Susquehanna River. In those days there was a large farm on the island, which I remember grew watermelon, cantaloupe. and other vegetables. If you could afford them, you could buy a melon for about 10 cents, or 20 cents if it was a large one. I don't remember that we ever did.

When Granddad and I stayed that week we didn't have a tent. My father cut some poles from the woods and made a kind of tent out of old tarps and canvas, tied them fast and then went home.

We fished on the point and caught one very large bass, and some other fish. Then we decided to fish at the cinder pile. Granddad always wore high boots, and would never take them off while he was fishing. Later I thought it was because he was so proud that he owned them. In those days they were a luxury item, a status symbol.

Sitting out on the cinder pile one morning, Granddad hooked a big one; a carp. Up the creek the fish went, down the creek Granddad went, and the fish dragged him out into the water. He had his hip boots rolled down to knee height. They filled with water and neither the fish nor Granddad would let go. What a great battle. I thought Granddad was going to drown for sure.

Finally the fish got off the hook. I have been wondering all my life how big he was. I saw him roll up to the surface of the water and he looked awful big to me.

Granddad didn't drown, but we talked about how big that fish was for a long time.

While we were at the river that week, I got a toothache. In those Depression years people didn't go to a dentist; you just yanked the tooth out. When my dad left us at the river we had a quarter between us. We had no medication along and my tooth was really aching. "We have a quarter," Granddad said. "There's a bar in town and we can get a shot of whiskey to kill the pain."

So we took off for the hotel where the bar was. The pain was still there and he got a shot of whiskey for 15 cents. I put some whiskey in my mouth, and Granddad said, "Don't swallow it, just keep it in your mouth."

Of course I didn't take much. I can't remember if it helped. "Can't waste it," Granddad said, since it cost 15 cents. So he drank the rest of it

Yes, it rained that week and naturally the tent leaked. But we both had a good time. At least I think we did.

# Fishing the Gut

In that part of the river, a little way downstream from York Haven was an area we called "the gut." The gut was a low-lying area that ran downstream along the edge of Brunner Island next to Conewago Creek. In the spring, rain and the river's ice flow flooded the area and fish followed the flow.

Local residents built rocks in a "V" shape, set a bushel basket or tub at the end of the V, and ate or sold the fish that ended up in the basket. After the spring flow of the river ebbed, the gut dried up and only small puddles remained. When the river flooded during the summer, the gut flooded too and washed out the stone V's. People would rebuild them for the coming spring flow.

Brunner Island was about three miles long, had railroad tracks and a steel bridge over Conewago Creek. Under the bridge, the creek had some deep holes where I spent a lot of time fishing after the spring flooding. We would catch mostly bass. While waiting for a bite we would cut driftwood with a hand saw, take it home and pile it in the cellar of our house.

Most of the island has changed. But the power company still uses the railroad, and the bridge is still intact. The company has built a large coal-fueled electric generating plant. The farm is gone, and in its place are large piles of coal and manmade lakes that were stocked with striped bass. At one time they sold these fish, but now you don't hear much about that. But I am told there are some still there.

For a number of years the island had a boat dock. Well, sort of. Someone drove stakes into the river bottom, built wooden planks out over the water, and had small wooden boats for rent that were about 12-16 feet long, with no motor but a set of oars. I can only remember renting them a few times. I can't remember the cost per hour, but I do remember that for a dollar you could stay all day, whatever that meant. One of our neighbors had a good union job, and if he came along fishing with us, we might get a boat.

Just below the island and north of York is a small town called Saginaw. I never did know if any industry was there or where people worked. The railroad tracks ran between the main street next to the river, and nearby all the houses sat in the back of the railroad tracks and the main street.

The road to Saginaw from York Haven remains to this day. It is still dirt or gravel, full of potholes, difficult to drive on, and you better not try to drive fast. It is a very lonely isolated area, just a few miles from York. Many stories exist concerning murders, attempted murders, rape and assaults. During the day, it's a nice, slow, pleasant drive. Go slowly and you may see a few fishermen along the way. I didn't fish the area often, and always only in the early spring.

## Exploring Near Safe Harbor Dam

Downriver from York Haven is Safe Harbor Dam. It was built in the early 1930s, and is the newest dam on the lower river. Construction was completed by thousands of workers. There were few protests during construction, as this was during the Great Depression. The shad and herring fishing was already destroyed by dams downriver and nearly everyone was looking for work.

The dam was built around an island, and constructed in two sections. The builders diverted the river around one side of the island and poured the concrete in that part. When they completed that section they ran water through the gates, which stayed open, to complete the other part. The actual power plant, which houses the water turbines, is on the Lancaster County side of the river.

This part of the Susquehanna is the closest to the city of York, and it is where I spent a lot of time along and on the river. When I was young Safe Harbor Dam was new and was just being explored. The changes were difficult to even begin to comprehend. Islands that once existed were covered with water and the canal and streams all changed.

One the earliest trips to the river I remember was to witness the burning of a house and barn on an island that was about to be partly submerged from the building of the dam. The island, which at the time was farmland, now belonged to the electric power company. It was a big occasion; a large gathering of people came to the hills overlooking the river to witness the fire.

Of course my dad had to see it, so the whole family piled into the car, and got into a traffic jam to watch the flames. It was quite spectacular and the crowd roared as the flames consumed the house, barn and other buildings.

No bridge connected the island to the shoreline. All the farm produce had to be carried across the water by boats and barges. It was a beautiful island, a few trees but mostly flat and rich farmland. It got flooded at times in the spring, which usually dumped more rich topsoil.

The part of the island that remains above water is now overgrown with tree vines. The back of the island is filled with mud and debris. Some years ago I tried to navigate around with a pontoon boat. I just barely made it to the lower end; I thought I was going to have to get out and push. But the muddy bottom was soft and the motor slowly churned its way through the mud as I got to the island's end and deeper water.

"I'll never try that again," I said to one of my cousins, Don Miller, who was with me. He nodded, though during that mile-long trip along the Lancaster County side of the island neither of us spoke. The island has a sandbar where it is very shallow, and many party boats anchor there. Some stay for the day, others stay for the night.

Because of flooding, which is usually severe every 10 years, and ice jams, the river bottom changes often. It is still good fishing if you use a fish finder and you find the channels that have an underflow and reach a depth of 11-12 feet.

Some years ago, Don and I were fishing near the island when he said, "I got a fish and it's a good size." As he reeled it in, I got the landing net ready and we got the fish aboard the boat. I don't know how long it took but it was the largest carp I've ever seen caught on the river. It was between three and four feet long, big and thick, full of raw eggs that filled the boat and we threw her back into the same area.

Years later I caught the largest blue catfish I'd ever seen. I was alone and thought I would never get it in. But I managed to take it in to shore. It was 32 inches long and weighed more than 11 pounds. To some people that may not be big, but for the Susquehanna River it was. A picture of me and the fish hung for a couple of years at the marina in Long Level where I kept my boat.

I caught a couple of walleyes over two feet long in the same area. I was sitting alone on the boat, a nice peaceful day. Around noon, which is usually slow, something grabbed my line. I pulled back but that never slowed him down. He just kept on going. The hook finally snapped off, and I will never know what it was.

Back when all the changes were taking place along the river during the dam's construction, few people I knew fished in that area. A section of the river, about five miles long, was known as Long Level. The farms along the river's edge were covered by the water. I do remember some of the old canal locks were not completely submerged by the dam. Most of the tow paths were still intact, and summer homes, bungalows and cabins were just beginning to arrive along the river. The first marina that sprang up was called the Long Level Marina, and it still exists to this day.

One of the first places we fished was a set of locks made out of stone. The stone house at the locks remained there for a number of years, but has been gone for some time now. The old barn and other buildings were destroyed long before the house.

The house was occupied by an old lady. She was known as the old lady by everyone — I don't remember anyone ever mentioning her name — and she owned the house and land around there, including the canal locks. Someone had built a footbridge across the canal lock walls and you could walk across two logs with boards nailed crossways.

The canal was filled with water, and we could fish the canal or the river. As a kid I liked to spend time catching sunfish in the canal, usually nothing big, but it was full of turtles, some of them snappers.

In my early fishing years, a state law forbade fishing on Sunday. The legislators of that time changed the law first to include daytime only, something like 7 a.m .to 7 p.m. The old lady evidently was somewhat religious and she became furious at the change.We ventured to the river to try Sunday fishing. But when we arrived, signs were posted saying "No Sunday Fishing." Since the land was private, believe me, we didn't fish there.

Later the law was changed saying people could fish all night on Sunday. But the old lady never changed her mind, and to get out to the river's shoreline we had to cross her footbridge. Since we didn't have a boat or money to rent one, we didn't fish that part of the river on Sundays.

At some point my family acquired a small tent called an umbrella tent. It had a center wooden pole with four metal hangers attached that swung out from the pole and fitted into the four corners of the tent. We then staked the bottom to the ground. We had to strap the pole on top of the car.

When our family of four wanted to go to sleep, we packed our gear in the car in case of rain, took out the bedding from the car, and dug a ditch around the tent to keep out water. If it was a nice day, we cooked and ate outside. Other times, we put our little camp stove inside and sat and ate. I can't remember having a table. But it sure beat the poles and tarps of earlier years.

Sometimes we carried the tent up or down the tow path, set it up by the river for the night, and fished all night and part of the next day. Most of the time we never knew when the dam would be filled or lowered, and sometimes water would come up into the tent. There were times we woke up soaking wet with stuff floating around in the tent.

Now we were wet and cold, so we needed to build a fire. There was always plenty of driftwood around, so we gathered a pile and got warm and dried off.

Depending on how many friends and family were along, the fires could get really big. If the crowd was large enough it meant two fires, and a competition to see whose fire could get to be the biggest. We built these big fires not only at Safe Harbor Dam, but at the Holtwood and Conowingo dams downriver also. The bonfires at York Haven were always smaller, probably because driftwood was more difficult to find.

One very cold spring day, we were fishing at York Haven out on the point, with a small fire burning. A neighbor was along that night, a real hothead. The fire was smoking quite a bit, and it seemed like every time he moved the smoke followed him. The neighbor got agitated, and kicked the fire into the river. I didn't have any say in this. Everyone waited and waited; no one said word. Finally the neighbor got out an old newspaper, doubled it up, got a few sticks of wood, and lit a new fire. Still no one said a word, and just continued fishing.

We caught minnows as bait fish in small seine nets. In the early years they were homemade. The net was about four square feet with strings attached to the corners. Then we found two small branches of a tree, tied them diagonally to the opposite corners so all four corners were tied. Then we put a bow in each limb, crossed them in the middle, tied the two together at the top of the bow, tied a piece of bread in the middle of the net with a string six or seven feet long to the top of the two limbs. You could catch your shiners while you fished.

We also used earthworms; we called them night crawlers. Most of them we caught at night out at a golf course in South York. It is now the campus of York College of Pennsylvania. Since the greens were watered during dry weather you could catch night crawlers all summer long. No one at the golf course ever questioned us, but then again we never damaged anything. The young kids in the neighborhood would go along with a flashlight. The reward for going along to catch night crawlers was often a trip to the river.

Once when I had a surplus of night crawlers I got the bright idea to put a sign up out front in the yard, which said "Worms for Sale." The sign said "10 cents per dozen." My older sister, Ann, really got upset. With my sister making all that fuss, I had to take the sign down. I don't believe I sold any.

I also had another problem — school. Dad or some other relative would tell me, "We are going fishing tomorrow, as soon as school is out." Sometimes a teacher told me I had to stay after school. When it came to fishing, no one could tell me I couldn't go. As the bell for the end of classes rang, I watched the teacher and as soon as her back was turned, I was gone. I left the consequences to be dealt with later.

When I got a note from school for my parents, and believe me I got a lot of them, I always gave it to my dad and somehow he took care of it. We never spoke about it. Even if one of Dad's friends wanted to take me without Dad, it was the same. We will take care of it later. I ended up spending a lot of extra time in school, but don't tell me I can't go fishing. Fishing was the most important thing in my life, and Dad in his own way let me do it. Right or wrong, Dad was on my side.

When Safe Harbor Dam was finished, before they closed the gates to let the reservoir fill, they cut down all the trees along the bank and the old canal tow path. Many huge tree trunks dotted the shoreline along the tow path and the river. Over the years as we learned where the best fishing was; we marked those spots by the tree stumps. We learned where we could catch bass, walleyes, catfish, and yellow perch.

During the early years of the dam, we didn't catch many fish. Then the state fish commission started stocking catfish, which we named spotted cats. You could catch 30 or 40 a day. Trouble was, they were only 8 to 12 inches long. We thought they would never get big.

We were wrong about that. I never did catch any 10-12 pounders, or any that were 30 inches long. But a lot of 15-20 inch ones are a really nice size for eating. They taste OK, but they ain't walleyes. However they are lots of fun to catch. Though for catfish I prefer large blues; the larger the head and mouth, the more fun to catch.

We fished on many cold days, but didn't use the soggy tow path as wet feet didn't feel good. One spot was along the shore of Long Level, which ran next to the old canal. You could drive along the river from Wrightsville about five miles to a creek. It had a bridge across it to a dead end. There was a house and a barn next to the river along the creek. There was a dock there where you could rent a wooden rowboat. I don't think they rented any motors.

At the mouth of the creek where it entered the river, the springtime brought good sucker fishing. They were a bony fish; the first fish you could catch in the spring. You couldn't, and still can't, catch night crawlers in early spring or late fall. So we fished with what we called garden worms. Suckers didn't care for large worms or night crawlers anyhow. It all worked out.

Of course fish didn't bite all the time. So I spent some of my time rearranging the stones, laying down outlines of houses and imaginary roads. One warm day, Mom, Dad and I were fishing along the tow path. Fish weren't biting too good, so I was moving rocks and stones. As I turned over a stone, a large snake came crawling out. It slithered up my pants leg, wrapped around my leg, and scared me half to death. I screamed and hollered, and Dad came running. I kicked and grabbed at my leg, the snake finally squirted out of my pants. I didn't build anymore stone houses down by the river for a long time; actually I don't believe ever.

# Burning a Bridge

Wrightsville was about as far up the river as the Safe Harbor Dam water went. Just below the town are three prominent islands. They are not real large but known by anyone crossing the bridge from Wrightsville to Columbia in Lancaster County.

A series of bridges across the Susquehanna have connected Wrightville and Columbia in Lancaster County for more than 200 years. The first was completed in 1814 and was the longest covered bridge in the world. It was destroyed by ice and high water in the winter of 1832. A second bridge was built and opened two years later. It too was a covered bridge more than a mile long with a tow path, one lane above the other, for the mules to tow barges and pass in either direction.

This bridge lasted until June 28, 1863 when Union forces burned the bridge to keep Confederates from crossing the Susquehanna during the Civil War.

The river was a significant geographical obstacle during the Civil War. Confederate troops captured York in late June of 1863. In order to take the state capital of Harrisburg, and move on toward Philadelphia, they had to cross the Susquehanna at Wrightsville. The Confederates set up artillery on the York County side of the river facing Columbia in Lancaster County. Militiamen gathered to block their advance. They were joined by Union troops retreating from York, and by a company of African American troops from Camp William Penn near Philadelphia, where the first black soldiers who enlisted in the Union Army were trained.

The big wooden covered bridge over the river was the prize the southern forces wanted. Outgunned and outmanned by Confederate artillery, the Union forces in Wrightsville retreated to Columbia and decided to use gunpowder to blow up a section of the bridge behind them.

According to an account in a blog by Scott Mingus Sr., "An unnamed 'old black man' had been patiently waiting on one of the piers to light the fuse. He had been calmly smoking a cigar while watching the distant activity in Wrightsville. He touched the end of his stogie to the fuse, made sure it caught fire, and then joined the exodus to Columbia."

The explosion failed to do the job, so Union forces set the bridge on fire, which collapsed and fell into the river. I grew up knowing the bridge was burned, but I was more than 80 years old before I ever heard a black man lit the fuse to try to blow it up.

The Confederates never crossed the river. The sole fatality of the skirmish that day was a black soldier, who was struck in the head by a shell fragment.

The current bridge between Wrightsville and Columbia, now officially called Veterans Memorial Bridge, was finished in 1930. It replaced an old iron-trussed bridge built in 1897.

My first remembrance of the old iron bridge was stopping on the York County side, waiting to cross. This was a one-lane bridge with a set of railroad tracks, with boards covering the railroad ties. The bridge was used by cars and trains. If a train came, the cars had to wait. It was the railroad's bridge, so trains always had the right of way.

When cars wanted to cross, they waited for cars coming from the opposite direction. The last one allowed on the bridge carried a round piece of wood, about 12 inches long and the thickness of a broomstick. It always reminded me of a baton in a relay race. When the last car arrived on the other side, the stick was handed to the first car crossing the other way.

Just south of the stone piers that carried the wooden bridge that was burned during the Civil War and the iron bridge, the new bridge between Wrightsville and Columbia was built out of concrete. It is a beautiful bridge, made with high arches, majestic in size and rising a great height above the river, and is still in use today.

I attended the opening day of this bridge, the first day motorists could drive across. It was two lanes with a sidewalk on the downriver side.

It cost a lot of money to cross and come back. The 25-cent toll was about a half-hour pay for those with a good-paying job. At the time you could you could cross a bridge into Harrisburg for 5 cents. Not a lot of people crossed that first day, but Dad said, "We gotta cross her" and we did.

Today there is another bridge south of Wrightsville, the Norman Wood Bridge, just below the Holtwood Dam. And there is another a short distance north of Wrightsville carrying traffic across Route 30. Years ago Wright's Ferry crossed the river to Columbia here. Even during the construction of the new bridge the ferry still carried people and vehicles across the river. It closed down around the completion of the new bridge in 1972.

# Upriver From Wrightsville

The river above Wrightsville has changed little since the years before World War II, while the land below the town was bought up over the years by the electric power company. While you can still own a cabin or bungalow, you can no longer own the land; you have to pay rent to the electric power company.

The land upriver was nearly all owned by a private landowner and still is, but lots of summer homes are located all over the riverfront.

Years ago, when Dad worked at the gas company in York, one of the managers was building a fairly large summer home along the river. Even as a young boy going down to work on the project with my dad, many items showed up that looked familiar to me from the gas works, as we called it. No one said a word about the origin of so many of these items that I had seen before in York. The swimming was good, as were the luncheons. It seemed there was always lots of food and drink to go around. These trips to the river upstream from the town of Wrightsville lasted all summer.

The fishing in the natural flow of the river during these summer days wasn't great, but getting a line wet was the most important reason for being out on the river.

Just up the river from Wrightville was a restaurant and inn called Accomac Inn, which still exists today. I never had the chance to dine there until long after World War II.

One year when I was a boy, I believe around 1936, brought a cold harsh winter. The Susquehanna froze solid. People began ice skating, then they brought ice boats with sails on them.

The winter got colder and people began to venture on the ice with automobiles. Dad heard about it and had to go look. There they were, out on the ice coming down the river full throttle. The drivers slammed on the brakes, and spun around and around like a top for miles. When they would get the cars stopped, they would do the same thing again. It was exciting to watch. Of course I wanted to go do it with our car, but Dad said no.

## Venturing Farther North

Goldsboro is a small river town just down the Susquehanna from Harrisburg. The shoreline below Goldsboro on the York County side is dotted with cabins, bungalows and summer homes. The Susquehanna is full of islands in that area, only accessible by boat; no bridge can take you out there.

Summer homes dotted every island. Everything taken out to the island was by boat. That includes building materials. But in 2016, Londonderry Township supervisors voted to approve an agreement with York Haven Power Company to terminate leases on the island.

I have never been on those islands. I fished nearby at the home of a neighbor's relative. I don't recall catching many fish, if any, and Dad and I only went back a few times.

Another area that always fascinated me is above Harrisburg; the Millersburg Ferry, which exists to this day. The wooden boats are built like barges with a paddle wheel in the stern. Today the ferry is more of a tourist attraction, but at one time it was used to take automobiles, supplies, crops and livestock across the river.

One other point of interest, about five miles north of Harrisburg, is the Rockville Bridge, the longest stone arch bridge in the world. That's right, in the world. It's a railroad bridge and trains still carry freight across it today. The bridge was built in 1902 and stood through the flood of 1933 and the one in 1972.

In the mountains north and west of Harrisburg, people mined coal, and hauled it to what they called coal breakers, washed it and let the water run into the streams that emptied into the river, bringing all the coal dirt into the Susquehanna and other rivers. Before there were regulations, stopping the practice was impossible. The first dam downriver, York Haven, halted much of the coal sediment. Above the York Haven dam, a number of barges dredged the river bottom for the coal sludge, which was sold for fuel.

That practice has been stopped and the debris from coal cleaning now flows into ponds. They still sell the coal silt today. Piles of it sit at Brunner Island power plant. But it's been years since I saw a coal barge dredging the bottom of the Susquehanna River.

## Holtwood Dam Cut Off Migratory Fish

Downriver from Safe Harbor is the oldest of three major dams below York Haven, now called Holtwood Dam. Construction began in January 1906, and the hydroelectric plant associated with it went online in August 1910.

I would like to mention one thing here: Native Americans used the Susquehanna to make a living long before anyone thought about dams and hydroelectricity. Much history is now at the bottom of the river, lost by the damming. I often wondered as my pontoon boat glided over a dam's water what might lie underneath.

Before Holtwood Dam, southeast of Red Lion, was built, shad and herring would migrate up the river, along with white and yellow perch. While the perch were not known as commercial fish, the shad and herring were. The building of the 55-foot high dam was controversial, according to my grandparents, who were alive at the time. They farmed in the Fawn Grove area, raising cattle, hogs and the usual grains grown during that era. They traveled the old Delta Road, now Route 74, hauling produce to York and grain to Red Lion.

My grandfather said that before the dam was built, they fished and netted the shad and herring. They would then bring them back to the farm and preserve them to eat during the summer. The area farmers also sold wagonloads of them to be eaten fresh or salted down for the year's supply of fish.

The story goes that when Pennsylvania Water & Power Company began building the concrete dam, many migrant workers arrived and camped along the river hills. They built a dirt road below where the breast of the dam was to be built. This caused the migratory fish to be cut off from their spawning area upriver. The locals decided to do something about it, and would sneak down to the river and use dynamite to blow holes in the road. Guards were brought in and a number of gun battles occurred. According to my grandparents, a number of people were killed, but no one could tell me how many and on which side.

On several occasions the locals also attacked and blew holes in the concrete dam itself while it was under construction. There was a meeting held and the power company agreed to put in a fish ladder. It was made of large stones and concrete walls, with the stones being laid in a system called riprapping. Water from the overflow dam, which was 60 feet high, was supposed to allow the fish to swim up and over the dam to continue their migration up the river, and move the young fish down the river to the Chesapeake Bay.

It never worked, and a new fish lift was built in the 1990s. If you get off the road right before the bridge across the river to Lancaster County, the old fish ladder is still there. You can see it from the gravel road.

There were also bonuses with this trip. A pair of eagles nested there for years and I could often see them from my car. Since the terrorist attacks of 9/11, security for dams and power plants has increased. You can no longer park there or visit the lookout over the dam breast, the fish ladder, or the eagles' nest, but you can drive by. Just before you get to the dam, an old lock from the inland water canal has been restored. Above and below the dam you can still find heavy iron pins driven into the rocks where fishermen used to net the fish.

Along the river at the upper end of Holtwood Dam were rocks and islands. This was a great area for bass and walleyes, and we had many a great catch. In that part of the river you needed a boat. Of course no one I knew had a motor when I was young. So we took the oars and visited the islands.

In that stretch of the river, a family opened a boat yard called

Gamler's. It was fenced in and had a swimming pool, small cabins and a boat launch area. Of course before World War II, I never got inside the gates.

Years later in the 1980s I rented space for a travel trailer here and had a pontoon boat. That is when I fished here, and it is one of the really interesting stretches of the river. But after having the travel trailer several years, never having stayed one night and having to launch my boat in and out of the water, I moved to another part of the river.

The Route 372 Norman Wood Bridge between York and Lancaster counties is only two lanes, high off the river, and offers a great view of the Holtwood Dam and the natural flow of the river and all its rocks.

Before 9/11, I often went down to the dam breast, where the water was between 40-50 feet deep at the gates. Access there is now prohibited.

There is danger in boating above the dam. The river flows over the breast of the dam. Boats have washed over the dam and crashed below; people have drowned. But the beauty of the power of the water flowing down the Susquehanna leaves me in awe of this great river.

Upriver from Holtwood Dam was Shenks Ferry. This was a ferry that crossed the river from the York County side to the Lancaster County side. Down next to the river was a small dock with a steep road where you could take your car or horses and wagons across the river. They also took cattle and pigs — and people sometimes. Across the road from the ferry up a steep set of steps was a country store. If you were lucky and had a penny and a nickel, you could get ice cream and candy. They sold everything you could think of; now there was a real country store.

In those days everyone was friendly and you were allowed to fish off the floating dock, many times all day and all night, as long as you stayed out of the way as the ferry was doing its business.

It was good fishing there and I don't remember ever failing to bring some home. The usual catch included bass, walleyes, catfish, carp, and yellow and white perch. In the early years the perch grew very large. White perch grew up to 12 inches and a few yellow perch grew 18-20 inches.

As the years went by the perch became extinct, and when the state began restocking them they never grew that large,; it seemed to me they never spawned as they did in the natural flow of the river. I no longer heard of anyone catching any migratory fish along the river.

Also along the river above Holtwood Dam, when the water level is lowered, you can still see Indian drawings — petroglyphs — on the rocks. Just above the dam is the Indian Steps Museum, which is a worthwhile visit.

As I travel many miles along the river now I find it is the same as it was when I fished those parts as a small kid. Little has changed in the last 80 years. Many of the summer cottages are small and seem the same.

# Conowingo Dam

Downstream from Holtwood Dam is Conowingo Dam; this dam was built between 1926 and 1928. U.S. Route 1 runs over the breast of the Conowingo Dam, and a drive across it is memorable.

But the dam stops silver American shad and herring cold. The migratory fish circle dumbly before the mystery of concrete. The shad fishermen and nets along the lower Susquehanna are gone.

In the 1990s, shad that arrived at the Conowingo from the Atlantic and the Chesapeake Bay were trucked above the four dams and released in spawning grounds above York Haven Dam. This effort met with some success, although to return to the Atlantic, the shad must swim through turbines in the dams, and some are killed. But the transport of shad was phased out after Conowingo, Holtwood and Safe Harbor dams built fish lifts, and York Haven built a passageway. These were largely failures and shad numbers plummeted again.

In 2016, Exelon, the energy company that now owns the Conowingo, signed an agreement with the federal government to upgrade fish lifts at the dam. Holtwood Dam is to improve its fish lift also, and York Haven Dam planned a new fishway. And the trucking of shad above York Haven is to resume in the latest bid to re-establish the shad fishery.

While Conowingo Dam is in Maryland, five miles south of the Pennsylvania state line, the water in the reservoir behind the dam is mostly in Pennsylvania. The dam backs up water for 14 miles, creating a 9,000-acre reservoir. Most of the fishing, and a lot of other things. are done in the upper end of the dam, just below the Holtwood Dam. The area is known as Peach Bottom.

This was a fascinating part of the river for a young boy prior to

World War II. It had islands and swift water, up to 90 feet deep. It had shallow areas where the boat would scrape on the rocks.

There was a boat-launching area called Boeckel Landing that had wooden docks and you could rent a boat for about a dollar a day. I didn't know anyone who owned a boat, so we all rented. Sometimes if the group was large enough, we would get two boats. We usually spent a day and a night out on the river, sleeping on the rocks.

The nearby islands had a few cabins, as we called them, and you could also rent a cabin from Boeckel Landing. We never did as we had no money. A few cabins were privately owned of course, but we didn't know any of the people.

One of the islands had a large rock formation known as Chimney Rock; everyone remembered it by that name. You could see it from quite a distance. The bass and catfish fishing there was great.

We came in early from fishing one afternoon and thought we would fish off one of the wooden piers at Boeckel Landing. The piers were fairly close to each other and a guy below us went to cast, missed his shot and the sinker hit a guy with us between the shoulder blades. He dropped like a stone. When he could finally talk, he said, "I would just as soon be shot between my shoulder blades." If it had hit him on the head it probably would have killed him.

Dad had a cousin Jake. They were friends and fished a lot together. Jake's wife, Martha, loved to fish, and most times went along. They had no children, so they kind of adopted me and took me along fishing. I loved to go along with them. Jake had a good steady job with the city, and they packed a great lunch and shared everything with me.

He found some humor in everything. We were down at Boeckel Landing once, just finished fishing. We were standing by the dock fully clothed and he said, "If I jump in will you follow?"

I said, "Sure." We ran down to the dock and we both jumped. As we waded out he just laughed and laughed.

Many nights and days we stayed on the islands and rocks out on the river. In the days before World War II, no one posted signs warning people to stay out so we would go out to one of the islands and pull up to a dock or deck if no one was home and spend the night sleeping on the island. Not once did we ever think of entering a cabin or harming or destroying anything. If someone was using a cabin we just moved to another rock or island.

It was a beautiful spot on the river. Every time you came around an island or inlet there was something different and beautiful. Great times on the river; no wars, no riots, and everyone respected other people's rights and property.

Jake, Martha and Dad taught me the fun of being outdoors. We didn't call it the environment back then, but we never left a mess. If we caught some fish, and I don't remember a time that we didn't, we kept them. We didn't know about catch and release. We kept the fish to eat, or give to a neighbor or friend to eat. I never remember counting them.

At another area upriver from Conowingo Dam, a couple of farmers had built two bathing houses. They were privately owned, but everyone could use them. Or at least, we did. Many times Dad's brothers, father, and family went to camp there.

At this time we still didn't own a tent, though Dad's brother did, and we all worked together cutting poles and building a v-shaped shelter. Usually we stayed a week; that was our vacation. Some of Dad's brothers would come down.

Granddad was always present. He was hard of hearing, never said much, didn't seem most of the time to know what was going on, but he was game for anything. You take him to the river, give him his fishing pole, and he was content. He could sit along the river, any bank or stream, never say much, just fish. I still recall two poems he would recite and I remember them both well.

As I look back, his life wasn't very pleasant. He lost his family during the Depression, never seemed to have a job very long, and worked on a federal program in Pennsylvania that put people to work. He died shortly after World War II with Alzheimer's disease; I didn't know what it was.

The times spent at the bathing houses with Dad's family were great. Everyone got along, I never heard an argument. While not all of them spent the week, you could rely on them showing up at some point. We caught all kinds of fish by the bushel basket. The big rock where Grandpa sat and fished is still there. In later years I often took a trip down to the site of the bathing house. I always think about what was, and always touch Grandpa's rock.

Several spots in this area were good for fishing. Two were down the river from the bathing houses. There were many old stone foundations from houses and barns that were torn down during the building of the dam. Fishing was always good at an old stone house near the shoreline, and in the cooler weather of spring and fall, the old stone walls made a place to keep warm where we could build a fire.

Farther down the river was a large rock formation that stuck out on the river. There was great fishing off "the rock." During one trip with a group of Dad's family we stayed all night on the rock. One day around daybreak, I was sleeping and Dad yelled, "You got a bite, he's pulling the rod in the river!"

I jumped up and hooked a big catfish. I was having difficulty handling it, and no one would help me as they stood around laughing. When I finally got it close to the rock I saw that it was a big blue-headed catfish. I remember thinking I could stick my fist in its mouth. They got the net and brought him in. How big he really was, I don't remember, but it was the biggest catfish we caught on that trip. We had a lot of fish that trip and one of Dad's brothers cut a wooden pole. They put the fish we caught, including mine, on it and with someone on each end carried them from the rock to the car at the bathing house.

Upstream from there were several good fishing spots, one being another old stone house foundation. Alongside the house was a small stream and we would build a little rock dam and keep the fish we caught in the pond it made before we took them home.

We lived in a friendly neighborhood in the northwestern part of York. The house we lived in had an outdoor spigot and a sink we would put a large washtub in. The sink worked off of a small stream of water and we would put the fish we caught in the tub and gave them away to neighbors. We didn't put carp in the tub; we would hang them up at the neighborhood grocery store, which had a roof over the sidewalk, and the large carp would soon be gone. I was told the Italians liked them.

## Traces of a Canal

Up the river from the bathing houses was a set of canal locks. During the 1800s the Susquehanna and Tidewater Canal operated between Havre de Grace and Wrightsville in York County. It was a hand-dug ditch along the bank of the river, built between 1836 and 1840.

Out along the riverbank workers constructed what was called a tow path from piling up the dirt that came from the canal and flattening it on top. Mules were used to pull the barges. The mules, and maybe some horses, were harnessed and hooked to towlines on the barge. Thus the name tow path. Each lock had a lock keeper who lived there with his family. The mules were stabled there and the crew stayed there if they needed lodging for the night.

Built out of stone, the locks were how canal operators raised the water level to take the barges up and down the river. Alongside the locks were a house, barn, and other buildings. They were nearly all made at least partially of stone. Most of these were torn down before I could remember, and the other parts of the canal, while not totally destroyed by that time, were in bad repair. There were breaks in some of the walls, which except for the stone locks themselves were made of dirt. The canal had filled up with mud and other debris.

In the backwaters in the spring time, the carp used to migrate for spawning and we could catch them by the hundreds with a landing net. Our nets were homemade with a round metal rim covered with net and with a broomstick attached. The broom handle was about four feet long, the rim and net were about 15-24 inches across.

On one occasion, I was standing along the stone wall of one of the canal locks and a big carp came swimming up. This was when I was about 10 or 12 years old. I reached as far as I could to put the net over his head and was going to try to pull him in. He went straight through the net and was gone. I didn't realize what could've happened. Had the net torn? I think he was bigger than I was and I could have been pulled into the water and drowned. I finally got the courage to tell Dad and he wasn't pleased. I'm not sure he believed what had happened.

Walking up the river to the next canal lock, it was a little different. The canal had filled in and the stone wall was out to the edge of the river. We would stay there at night to fish. The canal locks were usually more than a mile from each other so it was a long walk from one lock to the next. There was no road from the lower lock. But no one ever bothered us and we seldom if ever saw anyone.

As I learned years later, the next lock upriver was at the mouth of Muddy Creek. Yes, Muddy Creek is the correct name. This area nearly 12 miles upriver from Conowingo Dam has changed; today there are small cabins and bungalows. The canal has been filled in with dirt and a private road has been bulldozed out of the river hills and you can drive up to the creek. There is a public boat ramp, but I haven't fished that part of the river since I was a child.

Still farther up the river, just below where the Conowingo Dam water ends, down a narrow dirt road was a fellow who rented boats. He lived in an old wooden house in need of repair. He must have farmed at some time. The land had a barn on it, horses and some chickens. If the dam was low you could hardly get his boats in and out.

One trip I made with Dad's cousin Jake and his wife, Martha, the operators of the dam had the river pulled down, as we called it, and the water was swift and shallow. Lots of rocks were showing and Jake was trying to keep the boat off the rocks. He was rowing like crazy, when one of the oars skipped just under the water, hit a bass that was about two inches long, and it landed in the boat. Jack just sat there and laughed and laughed.

During World War II the United States developed the atomic bomb, which ended the war before I was shipped from the European theater to the Pacific. In the postwar era there were many stories about what we were going to do with atomic energy.

Some theories were an automobile engine that would run on atomic power by dropping in one small pill to power the engine until it was worn out. Or nuclear power would light and heat whole cities, and gasoline or fossil fuels wouldn't be used anymore. The Philadelphia Electric Co., later called PECO, got a permit to build an atomic power plant. The company decided it would be above the Conowingo Dam on the York County side of the Susquehanna, at the mouth of a stream an in area called Peach Bottom. Peach Bottom at the time had a hotel along the river's canal. I don't know when it quit operating but it was still standing after World War II.

The power company tore down the hotel, bulldozed the side of the river hills, and constructed the plant.

The building of the nuclear plant changed a lot of things along the river. New roads, bridges, and recreation areas grew along the river and most all of the land between the dams was bought up by the electrical power companies. People could still have a cabin, summer home or plot along the river. You could own the cabin, but you had to rent the land from the power companies.

Then restrictions came. People can still get to the river, but you put your boat in the river wherever the power company says you can. So far there isn't any cost, but the power companies built the boat launches and they decided where they are.

# The Lower River and the Chesapeake

As a young boy I fished the lower Susquehanna River and the Chesapeake Bay. Everyone could fish the bay and any tidal water of the Susquehanna without a license. Shad and herring were still being netted from the river. Men stood along the rocks on the riverbank with large nets with long handles, catching not hundreds but thousands of them.

In my early days, a Maryland town called Havre de Grace was a fishing village at the mouth of the Susquehanna River. At the time, if people got to know a boat captain, many would allow them to pitch a tent and stay by his boat landing. This one fisherman that our family knew allowed us to stay on his wharf, sometimes for a week. I remember he stayed on his boat all winter and the boat would be frozen in the water. I don't know how he stayed warm. I also don't know what we were doing down there in the winter.

In those days we cleaned the fish on the dock and dumped the remains into the river or the bay. The young fish would be swimming in those remains and feeding on them. Most of the fish, yellow and white perch, would eat out of your hand.

The dock was near the Havre de Grace bridge. At that time it was a double decker iron bridge. It was a single lane going in one direction, with the upper level going in the opposite direction. I was always fascinated with the form of that bridge, it was the only one like that I'd ever seen. During the early spring we always fished that part of the river. I know we always caught fish but I can't remember what they were. I believe they were perch, mostly white.

Nearby was another favorite fishing spot. For us, reaching it meant crossing the Conowingo Dam, which had a two-lane highway across the dam breast. It was the only bridge between Holtwood Dam and Havre de Grace. It was a narrow bridge, barely any room for two trucks to pass. In front of the road was the dam breast with huge floodgates. These were opened to control the dam level if more water flow than needed to to run the turbines came down the river.

During floods, crossing the dam was frightening, with the floodgates open and the water roaring through, bringing parts of boats, lumber, and large trees crashing through the gates over the dam, never to be seen again. Everything was completely crushed.

Just on the other side of the dam, the river made a sharp turn to the right, and several miles down the river was the Bainbridge Naval

Training Center. Prior to World War II the training center had several boat docks on the river and the living quarters were farther up the side of the river hills. In the early days you could fish anywhere, no restrictions, only a sign telling you it was U.S. Navy property. During the war it became an important naval training station.

I can remember fishing the tidewater here on the east side of the river in Maryland. I recall catching lots of fish.

## Making it to the River

Getting in and out of the hills along the Susquehanna was always an interesting trip. We never had any money; we were lucky to have 15 cents to buy a gallon of gas for the car. Yes, 15 cents to get us there and back. Seemed like the car's gas tank was always empty when we wanted to go fishing.

The dirt roads getting down to the river were a couple miles long, and in the spring they were muddy and full of deep ruts. Cars were much higher off the ground back then, the ruts were really deep and on many occasions in the spring everyone would pile out of the car and push it up the hill, motor revving and mud flying.

One spring day a neighbor who went along fishing with us a lot had driven his car. I don't remember what kind of car it was but it quit running and we were more than 15 miles from home. The adults figured out the engine wasn't getting any gas. Cars were much simpler in those days. They siphoned some gas from the tank into a tin can, and punched a small hole in the bottom. Dad lay on the running board that all cars and trucks had back then, and held the can over the carburetor and controlled the gas flow with his finger. We got out of the river hills and back to York with him riding on the running board.

When I was a teenager just prior to World War II, we moved to a farm in Glen Rock and the fishing stopped. I joined the Army and Dad spent all his time farming. Mother was helping with farm work, taking care of her father, and housing him and her brother, as they helped as farm hands. She had another brother who stayed at the farm at the beginning of the war. He had served in World War I and was too old for World War II.

After World War II, Dad began fishing again, and a few of my mother's brothers and relatives and friends went along. When I came back from military service I didn't have much time to fish. On a couple occasions before we were married, my wife, Sara, and I, and a couple of friends would go boating and fishing. After we married, we bought a farm, and had a family of four. I did very little fishing until 1990.

Things got a little better for Dad, and he bought a boat and a small outboard motor. He continued fishing down at Conowingo. A good friend of ours was Russ Amspacher, a blacksmith. He could build anything out of metal. Dad was having trouble with the propeller on the motor from being dinged by rocks in the river.

One day when Russ was along fishing, they hit a rock. Russ told Dad to pull the motor out of the water, took out his 24-inch ruler that folded to six inches, did some measuring in his head, didn't write anything down, didn't say anything. He went home and told Dad to bring the motor up to his blacksmith shop. He took a four-pronged fork and welded it to the motor. When Dad hit a rock, the fork pushed the propeller up and out of the water. It slid past the rock and back into the water and he never had to slow the boat down, just keep going for the next rock. Soon just about everyone had one in some way, shape or form. But the blacksmith never got it patented, never asked to be paid.

# Great Flood Changed the River

In 1972, a great flood brought on by Hurricane Agnes engulfed the whole Susquehanna River Valley. At Long Level, it destroyed nearly all of the cabins, bungalows, and summer homes, washing them away. Many boats floated down the river, through the Safe Harbor Dam gates, and crashed into the river below.

Destruction was everywhere. The old tow path was washed away for miles. The canal locks were torn apart, and many of the stones used to build them were gone. These were huge stones that I would never see again. One rock remains though; the one where Granddad Boyd fished.

The shoreline was changed forever and the Susquehanna itself was altered as well. What was once a huge long island is now split into two or three islands, and the water surrounding them is filled with mud and sand.

There remained some really deep holes in the river, some dipping 40 to 50 feet. One afternoon in the 1990s I was fishing off my pontoon boat in a hole about 40 feet deep when something grabbed my line. I jumped and began reeling in, and saw the big blue catfish. I netted him, brought into the boat and as I was admiring him, the other rod and reel was being pulled from the boat. I grabbed it and pulled in another catfish about the same size.

I brought them home and put them in the pond down at the farmhouse where we used to live. I often hoped someone would tell the story about the big catfish in that pond, but no one ever said a word. They should be a good size now.

# My Most Unbelievable Fish Story

Years ago I was fishing down at a deep hole at Long Level. A storm came up and it got really rainy and windy. I thought I better get up the river as I was several miles down from the marina landing. The waves were a good size for the river — two to three feet. When I got up to the marina the weather cleared, and since it was still early in the afternoon I thought, "Well, I'll fish a little."

I was sitting on the bench seat about halfway toward the back of the boat. Something grabbed my line and pulled my rod overboard. I had just bought it several weeks ago. I was really angry at myself, not at the fish, because I had never before paid half that price for a piece of fishing equipment. I couldn't believe I sat there and watched a rod and reel go in the river.

I didn't say anything to anyone, I guess because I was embarrassed for being so foolish. I went home still brooding, then I told myself it was only money, and I would just go buy another one and never tell anyone.

A couple of days later I went back to the river, fished several of my favorite fishing holes, and caught a number of fish. As I usually did, I checked the depth finder and moved back to the part of the river I had fished two days before. I sat for a while; nothing happened, no action. I was getting out of my boat seat when I got a small bite. I thought, "He doesn't amount to anything, I'll reel it in, then move and try one more spot before I go in."

I pulled back and felt something strange on the other end. As I reeled it in I found I had another fishing line on the hook. I got hold of the line, and began pulling it by hand. I felt something pulling on the line. As I got the line close to the surface I could see what appeared to be a fish. It let go. I kept on pulling the line into the boat and found a hook and sinker. I kept on pulling the line into the boat. When I got to the end there was my prized rod and reel.

If you don't want to believe this story, you don't have to. Sometimes I am not sure I do either.

Many people ask me how I caught so many fish. My answer is always the same: Be patient. You never know when it will happen. Decide what species you're after. Bring three types of bait that you know that species will usually bite on. Have a depth finder, or as some people call it, a fish finder. In my opinion, fish finders aren't important; their usefulness is showing the depth of the river, which helps you find the river's underwater channel. If you drop anchor and it sinks in the mud, the chance of the fish finding your bait is pretty small. Fish swim in channels, following the underwater current.

But I have no real secrets. If you want to fish for catfish you have to work at it. If you just want to throw a line in, that works too. The kind of bait you use is up to you; different days, different kinds seem to work best. The time of day usually makes a difference. The poorest time of day is noon until 3:30 p.m. Early in the morning and late afternoon are usually the most productive fishing times.

If your bait is old and waterlogged, put new bait on. Do you like old stale food? If you are too cheap to buy good bait, stay at home; you probably won't catch many fish.

For about a dozen years, I kept my boat at the Long Level Marina. I could take my boat down in the spring and then I was always ready to fish or boat. If I ran out of bait, they had some. Not a great selection but I could always fish.

Because construction of the dams on the lower Susquehanna stopped the natural migration of certain species of fish, they had to be restocked and it took many years for them to grow. I found that walleyes were not as plentiful as when I was a boy. Bass were the plentiful ones, both largemouth and smallmouth. Crappies and sunfish grew quite large out in the river.

I fished at least once a week during the season, and during a few years kept track of the fish I caught. In about a dozen years there was only one day that I caught only one fish. Two days I only caught three. Other times I caught 10 to 60 fish each day. Most fish I caught were catfish. Why? Because they are big and strong and put up a good fight, always heading to the bottom of the river. It's great fun if you hook a couple of 20-inch catfish at the same time.

Well, even two 15-inch ones aren't bad.

In later years, the only fish I took out of the river were catfish that I put in the Kiwanis Lake in York for the annual Labor Day Fishing Derby. One year I put 311 fish in the lake, all catfish.

On Labor Day young people, hundreds of them, compete for prize money and trophies. It's a great sight to see kids of all ages standing up, sitting down and throwing stones into the lake. Many are city kids who seldom if ever get to go fishing. It was always a good feeling to see a kid come grinning, bringing the fish to the contest table to be measured and counted.

# PART TWO — THE TRIBUTARIES

## Feeding the Susquehanna

Codorus Creek runs straight through the heart of the city of York, originating in the southern part of York County with branches flowing into a center stream before it enters the city.

One of these branches begins south of Glen Rock and west of Shrewsbury, on the farm where my wife and I raised our family. Farther downstream, where our brook ran into another larger stream, it became a creek that then flowed into the town of Glen Rock and branched out to New Freedom.

Our brook flowed into a farm anchored by an old stone house built prior to the Revolutionary War. This was the homestead owned by my mother's parents. The stream from the farm where my wife and I later raised our four children entered the larger creek in the meadow next to that stone house. As a boy I fished and swam in the creek in that meadow.

I remember Grandpa Miller, my mother, and dad, mowing the banks of the streams by hand with a scythe. Actually not just along the creek banks — the whole meadow, which was several acres.

An old farm lane crossed the creek to the fields on the other side of the meadow. There was no bridge to get across the creek. Instead my relatives built a kind of fort from rocks gathered from the fields to create a waterfall. The winter and spring rains often washed it away, so each spring, after plowing, the stones were loaded on a drag sled, which was built from two wooden beams about 6 or 8 feet long, with 2-inch-thick boards nailed to the beams. A metal ring fastened with bolts was pulled by one or two horses or mules through the field and the stones were hauled to the creek crossing to create the fort and waterfall.

Below the waterfall, a pool of water formed. I fished the creek often there, sitting many hours watching the water snakes lying on the rocks sunbathing, and sometimes catching a fish and eating it. I used to get angry at the snakes and throw rocks at them for taking the fish.

There was so much to explore in those years. One of my uncles was qualified as a mechanic and machinist. In those days no one in the rural areas had electricity. With the help of another uncle he built a wooden waterwheel, made a wooden chute, and the flow of water ran down the chute, turning the waterwheel. The waterwheel was attached to an old automobile generator, which charged some automobile batteries . The batteries were used to light the small gas station and candy store he had on the public road that ran through the farm. I thought it was interesting, but my focus was fishing. I didn't realize what a mechanical genius he was.

When I was a kid, no one posted signs on their land, and I had no idea what "No Trespassing" or "Private Property" meant. Back then we just respected other people's property. We never climbed over a fence, we went under it. We would tear our clothes before we damaged a neighbor's fence or property.

Every stream of any size along the Codorus had a dam or two. That stream was no different. One dam just downstream from Grandpa's farm ran a mill. Part of the dam breast and the mill race that ran the waterwheel to grind grain for food and livestock feed are still visible. A wooden bridge was added to the back of the mill, and a large steam engine ran the mill after the dam filled with mud and no water ran down the mill race.

The stone mill stands today and has been converted to living quarters.

Just below the old dam breast was a road that crossed the creek. Today it is a deep hole. I sat along the bank a lot; my uncle would take me to the waterhole, walk to Glen Rock, and let me fish until he got back from town. I don't know what he went to town for but it seemed to me he always said the barbershop.

I loved to fish and always caught a few, and sometimes a dozen or more. I always took them home to Grandma, who never said a word. She just cleaned them, no matter what the size. Sometimes people asked her, "Are you tired? Why don't you rest?" Her answer was always the same: "I'll rest when I'm dead."

I used to catch two kinds of fish in the creek, sucker fish and fallfish, which are also called silver chub. They were bright, silvery fish. Both species were small and full of bones.

Another dam was built downstream toward Glen Rock. It was originally built to create a pool to cut ice from in the winter using what's called an ice saw. The saw was about three to four feet long with large teeth. A stone building called an ice house was built nearby, and the thick ice slabs were stored in wood sawdust, which kept them cool in the summer.

The dam breast was built out of dirt, and had a spillway in the center, where water flowed over large rocks cut into squares. Soon after construction, the dam broke on the north side. It originally flooded the whole meadow, and has never been repaired in more than 80 to 100 years.

Farther downstream, in Glen Rock, two dams existed. One was on the branch of the Codorus that was diverted to the Glen Rock Mill to run the waterwheel. The dams are both gone now, one destroyed by flooding and the other by dynamite. As a young boy I fished both, catching mostly suckers and fallfish.

The mill race that supplied the water to power the mill ran under the streets of Glen Rock. If it hasn't fallen, the mill race runs a good block under the street's railroad tracks to the mill. The mill today is restored and is a restaurant. One room has a trickle of water flowing out of the rocks, which brings back memories and leads me to believe at least part of the race still exists.

The other stream from New Freedom accepted water flowing from the family farm. This stream goes under the railroad tracks, and under the road that goes back to the farm.

The New Freedom stream dam was across the street from one of the three barber shops in Glen Rock, where a haircut cost 25 cents. Nearly everyone in Glen Rock went ice skating during the winter on that dam. Sometime after World War II the dam was dynamited by state authorities.

Downstream from Glen Rock, a place called Centerville had a smaller stream that entered the Codorus. My grandfather told me of the days they built a V-shaped dam out of rocks, put a bushel basket just below it and caught fish to preserve them to eat in the summer. Downstream from there, more dams were built and I fished them all. Never fished anywhere I didn't catch anything.

All of the dams are gone from Glen Rock to Seven Valleys. Just below Seven Valleys was a great swimming hole — there was more to life than fishing.

# Where Branches Converge

Coming closer to York, the South Branch of Codorus Creek and the East Branch come together. At one time there was a dam just after the two branches of the Codorus joined, but it no longer exists. There is a road called Twin Arch Road, which runs under a railroad bridge. Prior to the 1972 flood following Hurricane Agnes, which wiped out portions of the railroad track, trains ran from Baltimore to York across Twin Arch Bridge.

If we parked at the bridge and walked upstream, we came to a stone-faced tunnel, Howard Tunnel. Just past the tunnel there was a mill dam where the fishing was good. It was a long walk so we seldom came in contact with anyone else. On one of the rare occasions my wife went fishing with me, we took another couple along. It was a pleasant day, we fished and caught a few; I don't remember the species.

Two dams were built on the East Branch of the Codorus. One has existed ever since I can remember. We always knew it as the York Water Company dam. Today it is known as Lake Williams, built in 1913. This was all private property and when I was a boy we could not fish, boat, hunt, or get on the water.

However, there is a public road built over the dam. They could not keep us from fishing off the road. We could fish from the bridge along its concrete abutment. But don't get on the land. Right beside the road was a house where the dam attendant lived, who patrolled the lake in a rowboat. He was a big man and ruled with an iron fist. I don't remember ever seeing anyone on the dam.

Boys often rode bicycles down to the dam and fished all night. I remember one hot night early in the morning, a friend jumped off the bridge and swam to a bridge pier and got out before the big guy showed. The fishing was really good, with largemouth and smallmouth bass, white perch and a few yellow perch, bluegills, sunfish, a few crappies, and silver carp. Many times you could see the fish come to the breast and turn around and swim back into the lake.

The upper end of the reservoir was crossed by the Susquehanna Trail. The bridge then was an old iron structure; a beautiful bridge. Dad and I were sitting along the bridge fishing one afternoon and a car came down the road really fast and got to the curve on the road. A truck was in the middle of the bridge and the driver of the car slammed on his brakes. Spinning and swerving, somehow he did not wreck. He stopped, got out, and we asked if he was all right. He turned around and said, "Check my pants, if they aren't stained I'm OK." We went back to fishing and everything went back to normal.

But road clearance under the bridge was low so a truck with an overly tall load had to find a way around. Later I bought a wooden shed, and it was being delivered on a flatbed truck. He couldn't get under the iron bridge.

That bridge has been torn down and replaced with a new concrete span. Above the new bridge and the old dam, the water company built a new reservoir in the 1960s called Lake Redman. Some years ago the water company agreed with the county and state government to declare it a county park. They then opened the shoreline to public fishing and hunting, including some public boat ramps. I haven't fished it so I have no fishing history there.

Upstream from Lake Redman, the York County government bought more than 800 acres and named it Spring Valley County Park. The East Branch of Codorus Creek flows through it, and is stocked with trout. I never fished it but went over there to catch live minnows to fish the Susquehanna. It's a nice area to drive through, with horse riding trails and many trout fishermen. It's a pleasure to just stop and watch the trout in the pools of water. I just never got into trout fishing

The area is also called Rehmeyer's Hollow, and since long before it became a county park in 1972 and was renamed there has been a tale associated with it. Nelson Rehmeyer was thought to be a witch doctor, or as the Pennsylvania Dutch called them, powwow doctors, who could cast spells, or hexes, over people. In 1928, one of his neighbors, John Blymire, was having difficult times and was told by another powwow doctor that if he got a lock of Rehmeyer's hair and his spell book and buried or burned them, his troubles would go away.

Blymire and two teenagers went to Rehmeyer's home to try and rob him and get a lock of hair. Rehmeyer resisted, was killed, and they tried to set fire his body. The house didn't burn and the three were convicted and served prison time. The house still stands about 90 years later.

After the murder the hollow stayed pretty much underdeveloped for many years, before it was purchased by the York County government. The area is beautiful and uninhabited. Many contributing streams enter the East Branch of Codorus Creek here. It's a natural place and home to beautiful wildlife. Many of the roads through it are unpaved.

Not many people go there, but visitors who do can drive through miles of wilderness just south of York, nearly to the Maryland-Pennsylvania state line. Or they can spend hours walking, horseback riding and in certain areas find a pond to fish in. It is a vast park so there are no huge crowds fishing in one hole.

There are not many people driving fast to pass you with dust flying. If you go there, don't be in a hurry. If you like wilderness and nature, it's available free in York County.


# Codorus Becomes the Inky Stinky

Codorus Creek and the city of York are inseparable. You can't talk about one without the other. The creek has been known by a number of names, including the Inky Stinky. But it must have had some redeeming features if so many people flocked there and stayed there. The settlers who founded York in the 1740s didn't discover Codorus Creek; long before that American Indians lived along it. When the settlers did arrive, they stayed along the Codorus, built factories and houses. The creek was the center of the city. Several dams existed and were used to supply water to industries.

Many people blame the creek's pollution on paper mills, which certainly were a part of it. Years ago at least three paper manufacturers were in operation along Codorus Creek. The wastewater from all three flowed through parts of York. P.H. Glatfelter's Spring Grove paper mill still discharges wastewater into the Codorus. But in reality the problem was more complex than that.

As a young person I remember sitting along the creek's banks in York. In the late 1920s and early 1930s I don't recall it smelling bad.

You could fish and the banks were dirt, not stone, with a few trees along the creek.

But here are things I saw happening without understanding. Many downtown properties ran their sewage directly into the creek. Toilet paper, among other things, would sometimes be seen floating downstream.

Every so often fish would come floating by, many dead and others very sick. York County Gas Company was along the creek. It had a freshwater pond on the premises; we used to get the sick fish from the creek and put them in the pond and keep them there until they recovered. Not all of them did.

Other small streams in the city sometimes had fish in them. On many occasions the streams cleared and fish came back. Whatever caused the pollution cleared but always returned and became worse over time. Not too long into the 1980s, it was discovered that some wastewater pipes never were connected to the sewage plant.

There were also many factories along the creek; not nearly as many now as there once were. The worst polluters are gone, but some remain.

In recent years there has been new interest in the Codorus. Much of the polluted soil is being cleaned and a great deal of money is being spent to make it a clean stream where people can sit along the banks, catch fish, and not be afraid to eat the fish.

One of the factories along the creek on the east side of the city was the York Safe and Lock Company. It employed hundreds of people. One of the boroughs surrounding York is North York. It was separated from the York Safe and Lock Company by the Codorus. Many workers lived across the Codorus from the factory, which built a swinging footbridge so workers could cross the creek and enter the front gates of the plant. It was never rebuilt after a 1933 flood.

I never fished in Codorus Creek downstream of York as it flows to the Susquehanna. I have only travelled along the banks. During the Depression years of the 1930s, Works Progress Administration workers built a trail down the north side of the creek. It had small wooden bridges across streams that entered into the Codorus. I am not sure how far it went downstream from the city, but it was several miles. It was a nice footpath. It since has been destroyed; the bridges and the path are gone. It too could have been destroyed by flood.

# Park Created From West Branch

The West Branch of Codorus Creek begins in the southwestern part of York County, in the Hanover and Spring Grove area. About 60 years ago the area near Hanover and south of Spring Grove along a stream was known as Marlboro Flats. In the 1960s someone began buying up all the farms in that watershed area. No one seemed to know who or why. The more farms that were bought, the higher the price for those remaining. Eventually all were purchased.

Driving down Route 216, the road between Hanover and Glen Rock, I began to realize no one was farming the farms. This was thousands of acres.

P.H. Glatfelter Co., which operates a paper mill in Spring Grove, was buying the land. The paper mill needed a source of water. Glatfelter built a huge dam and flooded thousands of acres. After all the approvals from the state and federal government, the company made the announcement that would turn nearly all the shoreline of what was named Lake Marburg into a state park. All the company really wanted was the reservoir of water.

The area became known as Codorus State Park. The state stocked the lake with some of the finest fish that would adapt to the area: Bass, pike, crappies, bluegills, walleyes, muskies, and a whole bunch of others.

The state built a number of docks and people can dock their boats all season or launch at some smaller boat landings. You may find ice fishermen on the ice when it is thick enough to be safe. The park has a large swimming pool and camping is permitted in certain areas. I have only been out on Lake Marburg once, in a boat with my dad. I bought a small aluminum boat for Mom and Dad after they could no longer go fishing in Ocean City, Maryland. Of course, it had an outboard motor. But in less than a year he bought a small electric motor. They both enjoyed it for a number of years.

The water from Lake Marlboro flows into Spring Grove to the paper mill, and then into York. The water from the paper mill was once badly polluted. The water is still discolored, but has been cleaned up and only has a little smell. When the Codorus reaches the Susquehanna, it has little effect on the water quality of the river.

# Exploring Conewago Creek

My familiarity with the Conewago is about 10-12 miles from York through Manchester to York Haven. The creek flows from the west to the northeast in York County, north of the towns of Dover and Strinestown. My father-in-law, Emory Strine, who was raised in Strinestown, often told me of netting migrating shad and herring in the Conewago.

A tributary, the Little Conewago, runs into the Big Conewago between Manchester and York Haven, where the creek then flows into the Susquehanna.

The Dover Trolley Line stopped at two different parks on the way from York to Dover. One was on the Big Conewago and one on the Little Conewago. The bridge over Route 74 crosses upstream from the original bridge over the Big Conewago Creek. After you crossed the original bridge, you turned left and there was the road that closely follows the creek. There I fished many times for bass, suckers, and carp.

I have a fish story from this area that seems unbelievable. While fishing as a young boy, I had a bite and hooked a fish. While I was reeling it in, the line tore and I lost him. I put on new hooks and kept on fishing. Later in the day I had another bite. I reeled the fish in and my original hook, line, and sinker were all in its mouth. I don't remember how big it was, but it must have been a good size.

Sometimes late in the spring, the fish wouldn't bite in the muddy water. So we would go upstream from the fishing hole, cut a wooden pole, stick it in the creek, stir it back and forth, and the fish would begin to bite downstream. When the water cleared upstream, the fish would quit biting and we would go back up the creek and stir the mud up and catch more fish. It didn't work in the summer when we were fishing for bass.

A concrete bridge on Route 181 now crosses the Conewago between Manchester and York Haven, but the old iron bridge is still intact and stands just a few feet upstream from the new one.

Just before you get to these bridges, a road turns upstream and passes two concrete pillars where the old trolley line from York to York Haven stood. The trolley tracks were very high and dominated the skyline. We fished both sides of the creek, usually near these pillars.

One side of the creek had bungalows along the bank, and the other side was open space like a park. The fishing was good; we were always able to catch something.

Late summer was bass fishing. People drove in, parked the car and began fishing. No one seemed to care, and everyone respected the other person's property.

Back on the road from Manchester to York Haven, just north of the creek was the Conewago Inn. It stands today and is still in business. Just upstream from the trolley line pillars, the road makes a sharp turn to the right, crosses an old one-lane iron bridge, and becomes a dead end. The area is where some of the most scenic pictures in that part of York County are taken.

Going downstream toward the Susquehanna Trail stands an old stone mill. After it was no longer being used as a mill, it was converted into a bar and inn, and later to apartments. The mill dam across the road was gone long ago.

## Along Little Conewago Creek

When I lived in the northwestern part of York, I spent a lot of summers on Little Conewago Creek between Route 74 (Dover Road) to Bull Road. We often hiked out from York or rode our bicycles.

Nearby, one of my friend's uncles had a dairy farm where he bottled milk. We sometimes stopped there for a drink. At the bottom of the hill was the Little Conewago. We fished there often, and on occasions pitched a tent and stayed the night. A doctor had a big house on the hill. We crossed the creek on a low cement bridge with four pipes running through it. We camped in the doctor's meadow beside the bridge, never asking him before we did. In my early days, that's what kids did.

On the lower side of the bridge was a fairly deep fishing hole. This is where I learned at a very early age how fish bite, and how they swam in schools. The water was usually clear all summer long, except after a rainstorm. We could set our bait, usually a worm or night crawler, as it floated in the current.

The fish most always swam in schools. I learned that one would strike the bait and if it let go a second, third, or fourth would bite. It usually wasn't the same fish. The fish were small, but the pattern was usually the same. I believe watching those fish taught me a lot about catching them.

One night while camping along the creek a fierce thunderstorm came up; rain, thunder, and lightning. We left the tent and went into the doctor's barn for the night. We didn't ask, and no one said anything. The next morning, we cleaned up the wet mess in the tent and stayed a few more days.

On one of our trips we were fishing just up the road from the doctor's house. A farmhouse and barn were along the creek. Somehow while I was carrying my rod and reel I got a fish hook caught in my leg above my knee. It was stuck in there, right above the barb of the hook, and I couldn't get it out. The farmer was out at the barn and I asked him if he could help. I sat down in the barnyard and he said he'd take a look. Because it was stuck between the barb on the hook and the eye for the string, it wouldn't come out. The farmer — I never knew his name — got pliers, cut the shank off near the hook's eye, and pulled it through. He put some ointment on that he used for horse injuries. I thanked him and went back to fishing.

When I got home I showed it to my mother and dad. They just looked, and I never went to the doctor. I had heard of lockjaw, but didn't have a clue about a tetanus shot. And I wouldn't have had any money to go to the doctor anyway.

Down the creek from the doctor's place was Bull Road. Just a few hundred feet upstream from the Bull Road was a bend in the creek, and a deep hole. Someone had put a diving board on the creek bank and lots of people used it to swim. Some of my friends who didn't care much about fishing went along to the creek one day and began swimming. One kid was playing on the diving board. Then he began hanging from it. One of the boys began trampling on his hands, and he yelled "I can't swim!" but the other boy just stomped on his fingers harder and harder. Finally, he let go and swam out of the water. I have no idea what anyone would have done if he really hadn't been able to swim out.

Downstream from Bull Road was a mill dam that backed water up near the swimming hole. An old wooden covered bridge crossed the road. Most creeks had covered bridges at that time. All of them were made of wood, including the wood-shingled roofs.

In winter, we often went ice skating here. The dam slowed the current so the creek froze most of the winter. Usually we built a small fire on the ice and spent hours on the dam.

When spring came, the fishing began and the sooner we could start, the better. One year it was early April, around Easter week. One of the issues that came up each spring was who would be the first guy to take his clothes off and jump in the creek. There was one guy who usually won; he was the one who also dove off the bridge at the water company impounding dam. We dove in, didn't stay too long. I don't remember if we caught any fish but it didn't matter; we were fishing. That's what was important.

Upstream at Route 74, the road to Dover crosses the Little Conewago. Up there was a dam and a mill where I never fished, but downstream the Little Conewago ran through Grandview Golf Club.

The creek wasn't very deep in this area and we used to catch minnows for bait to fish in the Susquehanna at York Haven. We used to use a net to catch small catfish. We called them stone cats and they were great walleye bait. They were about two inches long, and to find one that was three inches was rare. But the walleyes loved them, and that area of the creek on the Grandview golf course was the only place I could ever remember catching them — above the Route 74 bridge and never below the golf course. I don't know how or why they were there. We caught a lot of them though. They were tough, lived a long time, and I hardly ever had a walleye get one off the hook without catching him.

The other thing we could net in this stretch of the creek was golf balls. We used to get a lot of those.

One time downstream from the golf course, just below the property line, I caught a decent size catfish. The fishing was bad that week and we had a big celebration. It wasn't a real big fish, but it was a welcome one.

Brookside Park, at the edge of Dover, was originally built by a trolley company to boost ridership on weekends. It had a merry-go-round and several other rides, a picnic area, and a band shell. The rides are gone now. But back then, during warm weather open trolleys ran to Brookside Park from York. The trolleys had no doors or windows and were only used during the summer. I never heard of anyone falling off or jumping off.

We did a lot of early spring fishing on the Little Conewago in that area along Canal Road. Just before you came to the Susquehanna Trail was another area where we used a wooden pole to muddy the water. If the fish weren't biting, it really worked.

Between Dover and the Susquehanna Trail a wooden bridge crossed the Little Conewago at a small unincorporated town called Foustown. There was a dam and a mill with a water wheel upstream from the road. We spent a lot of time there as it was within bicycling distance of the city. Above the dam breast was a deep hole and someone climbed a tree and attached to a limb what we called a hay rope, which was used in a barn to pull the loose hay up in the barn's haymow to be stored and used as feed for the cows and horses during the winter. The rope was tied to a limb of the tree with a knot at the end, and hung over the water near the dam breast. We used to swing out over the water, let go, and crash into the water. There was also another tree whose branches hung over a steep bank and we would dive off that.

After floods in the 1970s, the dam broke and the whole area changed. The old mill was converted into living quarters.

The old mill dams made for excellent fishing, and if the fish weren't biting you could always go swimming. You seldom if ever saw a "No Trespassing" or "No Swimming" sign.

One dam still exists on the Little Conewago where it flows under Bull Road. On a sharp curve on the right going toward York was a large stone store with gas pumps, where we would stop and buy a bottle of soda for a nickel, if we had one. If we had two nickels we could get a candy bar too. The building is still there, but the gas pumps and store are gone; it is now a private residence.

The dam has partially survived. Though the toll of flooding and high water has left a deep washout, it is good to see the dam is still there. Many private bungalows or cabins still dot the area with small docks and boats, just north York. One thing has changed though: "Stay Out," "No Trespassing," and "No Fishing" signs are everywhere. I never did much fishing on the dam, but you bet I got my line wet on occasion.

## Adventure Away From the Water

As a young boy maybe in first or second grade, some friends and I heard there was a large cave near West York. Early one morning we went prepared to enter the cave. The entrance was a little above and north of my house. We brought little candles (who could afford a flashlight?). It was time to explore.

We assigned the smallest and youngest kid to stay at the entrance. The other three of us decided we would begin the exploration. We told the little guard at the entrance to stay there, not to go anywhere, and if we called he should answer. We entered a fairly large room, lit our candles, and entered a narrow passageway and came to a larger area with a long stone ledge.

We explored for a while and then got disoriented. A little candle didn't make much light, and as we got farther back, we couldn't keep the candles lit. It was an exciting and fascinating adventure, but we wanted to find our way out. First we called, then we hollered. We hadn't told anyone what we had intended to do, and when no one answered we panicked. The faster we moved, the faster the candles went out.

The cave had a number of different directions and turns. It was interesting and beautiful, but now we were very scared. Finally, we saw a little light. It seemed to be above us. We saw a shelf in the cave and climbed up and crawled along the ledge. We didn't know if we were going toward the entrance that we came in or going back farther into the cave.

As we crawled along the ledge we came to a large room. We discovered it was the one we had first entered through. When we got out, the younger boy told us he got bored and walked away. He was sitting down and playing in the dirt when we found him.

In later years when I told the story, people who knew of the cave claimed it runs from the entrance toward Rutter's farm and dairy, off the Susquehanna Trail. Over the years housing and commercial development began to cover the area. If the direction of the cave is correct, someone's living room could be right on top of it. One thing I do know; I never went into the cave again. Today the entrance has been sealed off. Whenever I pass the entrance I still wonder what it would be like to go back inside.

Incidentally we didn't need our fishing equipment that day. We got on our bicycles and went home. I never told my family. Thank goodness they didn't ask so I wouldn't have to tell.

# A Spot Along Muddy Creek

The north branch and the south branch of Muddy Creek come

together at Muddy Creek Forks. From there Muddy Creek flows though Woodbine in southern York County on its way to the Susquehanna.

Entering a deep gorge down to Muddy Creek, a concrete arch bridge crossed the creek. Just below the bridge was a cement dam built for an electric generating plant. It was in shambles when I first began fishing the creek. Anyone looking for the dam, the bridge, and the power plant now will be out of luck — they are all gone. A new concrete bridge now takes State Route 74 across the creek. By the time Muddy Creek flows under Route 74, it is fairly wide waterway.

I don't recall ever fishing below the dam, which backed up the water quite some way along woods and pastureland. The early spring and late fall were great times to catch lots of fish here, and bring some home to York. These were Depression years, and we would feed our whole city block, or at least those who wanted to eat fish.

After we parked the car along the road, we took a long path to our favorite fishing hole. Each person had the special spot where they fished from. Once one of our neighbors was along with Dad, Mother, and me. Mother didn't bother to pick a choice spot, just cast her line in. We were all sitting close to each other and Mother got the first bite. Then the second. Then the third and so on.

Our neighbor didn't even get one bite. Mother made the mistake of saying, "There's fish where I am, I'll move." Our neighbor didn't answer, just reeled in both of his lines and sat on the bank. He didn't say, "Let's go home." He just sat there. We stayed most of the day before we finally took our fish and went home. No one said a word the whole way home.

There was a small settlement on Muddy Creek called Castle Fin. It still exists today, but during a flood caused by a hurricane in 1933, the bridge there washed out and we couldn't cross the creek as we had in earlier years. I never cared to fish there after the flood; I always thought the fishing hole on the opposite bank, which was no longer accessible, was better.

As the years went by, we seldom fished Muddy Creek. The old covered bridges were all replaced with concrete. That seemed to change everything. I guess I remember it sentimentally. It's been years since I fished Muddy Creek. It is still a beautiful area to visit once or twice a year. The roads are better and the area has changed; things don't seem to be as rural and unspoiled as they appeared during my early years.

One thing hasn't changed. Muddy Creek is still a twisting, winding, stream that always kept me wondering if I was going east or west, north or south, and to this day I wonder what I'll find around the next curve.

It's still beautiful. And so is the Susquehanna and all of its tributaries.

# AFTERWORD

Dick Boyd celebrated his 93rd birthday shortly before this book went to press. His most recent fishing trip on the Susquehanna was on a charter boat with family members in the summer of 2016, when he pulled in some catfish north of Wrightsville and Columbia. He suffered a fall a few months later and no longer explores the Susquehanna on his own, but still visits the river and its tributaries with family members.

My father put his recollections about the river and its creeks on paper over the course of a decade. Thanks go to my godson, Donald Shubrooks, who patiently turned Dad's handwritten notes into a typed manuscript, and to my son, Matt Boyd, who gave the text its final edit, organized the manuscript, designed the cover and worked with the publisher to get it into print.

I also pass on here the gratitude Dad has expressed to my siblings and their spouses, Becky and Dick Rishel, Nick and Donna Boyd, and Beth Thames, for helping our parents as their incredibly active lives have slowed in recent years. Thanks to my wife, Katy, for her patience and help as well, and to Dad's grandchildren and great-grandchildren for returning the love and kindness my parents have shown them throughout their lives.

And all of those mentioned above join Dad in expressing love and gratitude to Sara Boyd, whose patience Dad has tested for more than 70 years. We all know that our family ties would not be so close-knit without her.

Rick Boyd,
Oct. 5, 2017

# APPENDIX

For several years, Dick Boyd recorded how many fish he caught from his pontoon boat each day he went to the Susquehanna River.

## 2006

| | |
|---|---|
| April 25 | 23 fish |
| May 1 | 12 fish — also lost rod, reel |
| May 3 | 9 fish |
| May 6 | 6 fish |
| May 9 | 9 fish |
| May 19 | 1 fish |
| May 26 | 7 fish |
| June 8 | 22 fish |
| June 12 | 14 fish |
| June 19 | 14 fish |
| June 24 | 23 fish |
| July 6 | 21 fish |
| July 7 | 26 fish |
| July 10 | 25 fish |
| July 14 | 12 fish |
| July 17 | 19 fish |
| July 20 | 28 fish |
| July 21 | 45 fish |
| July 28 | 5 fish |
| July 31 | 20 fish |
| Aug. 4 | 6 fish |
| Aug. 11 | 34 fish |
| Aug. 24 | 15 fish |
| Aug. 29 | 26 fish |
| Sept. 6 | 36 fish |
| Sept. 8 | 18 fish |
| Sept. 9 | 30 fish |
| Sept. 17 | 22 fish |
| Sept. 22 | 8 fish |
| Oct. 3 | 19 fish |
| Oct. 9 | 19 fish |

I caught 8 bass and 5 sunfish in 2006. The rest were catfish.

## 2008

| | |
|---|---|
| April 24 | 41 fish |
| May 2 | 22 fish |
| May 6 | 38 fish |

By June 30, 2008, I put 174 fish I caught in the river in Kiwanis Lake in York, stocking up for the Labor Day fishing tournament for kids.

## 2009

| | |
|---|---|
| April 24 | 9 fish |
| April 30 | 5 fish |
| May 4 | 29 fish |
| May 10 | 40 fish |
| May 22 | 14 fish |
| May 24 | 7 fish |
| May 24 | 8 fish |
| June 1 | 7 fish |
| June 6 | 8 fish |
| June 11 | 12 fish |
| June 14 | 7 fish |
| June 18 | 10 fish |
| June 26 | 10 fish |
| July 7 | 2 fish |
| July 12 | 4 fish |
| July 14 | 13 fish |
| July 20 | 10 fish |
| July 23 | 3 fish |
| Aug. 1 | 3 fish |
| Aug. 8 | 1 fish |
| Aug. 13 | 10 fish |
| Aug. 31 | 7 fish |
| Sept. 7 | 7 fish |
| Sept. 17 | 7 fish |
| Sept. 21 | 7 fish |
| Sept. 24 | 6 fish |
| Oct. 3 | 2 fish |

By Oct. 3, 2009, I put 165 fish I caught in the Susquehanna in Kiwanis Lake in York, Pa.

Made in the USA
Middletown, DE
11 July 2021

44005392R00031